COMPANY TOWN

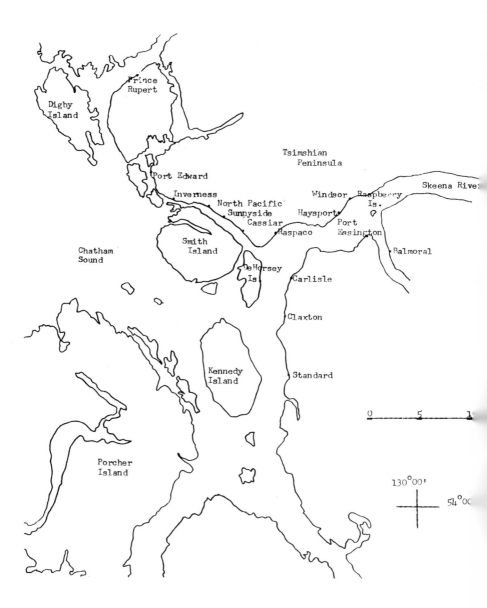

Digby
Island

Prince
Rupert

Tsimshian
Peninsula

Port Edward

Inverness

North Pacific

Sunnyside

Cassiar

Maspaco

Windsor
Raspberry
Is.

Skeena River

Haysport

Port
Essington

Balmoral

Chatham
Sound

Smith
Island

DeHorsey
Is

Carlisle

Claxton

Kennedy
Island

Standard

0   5   1

Porcher
Island

130°00'

54°00

COMPANY TOWN

MICHAEL TURNER

PULP
PRESS

VANCOUVER

COMPANY TOWN
Copyright © 1991 Michael Turner

Published by
PULP PRESS
Arsenal Pulp Press Ltd.
100-1062 Homer Street
Vancouver, B.C.
Canada V6B 2W9

The Publisher gratefully acknowledges the assistance of
The Canada Council and The Cultural Services Branch,
B.C. Ministry of Municipal Affairs, Recreation and Culture.

Printed by Hignell Printing
Typeset by the Vancouver Desktop Publishing Centre
Printed and bound in Canada

CANADIAN CATALOGUING IN PUBLICATION DATA
Turner, Michael, 1962–
  Company town

  Poems.
  ISBN 0-88978-235-0

  I. Title.
PS8589.U76C6 1991   C811'.54   C91-091444-3
PR9199.3.T87C6 1991

CONTENTS

CANNERY CUT

WHERE THE FISH
ARE NEAR FRESHEST

POEMS FOUND AT SEA

Mary tells me she admires the salmon
because it is such a romantic fish.
It travels two thousand miles in order to spawn,
then dies in a ritual of love and death,
its flesh feeding new generations.

—*Elizabeth Brewster, poet*

There are still men and women among us
who were active participants
in the life and struggles
of primary resources frontiers
of one, two, and three generations ago.

—*Rolf Knight, anthropologist*

When this place goes under nobody'll notice the diff'rence.
Nobody, that is, 'cept the people who spent their lives workin'
here. I take no pride in bein' part of the last generation of Skeena
River cannery workers.

—*Eddie Holton, fish butcher*

INTRODUCTION

THE NORTH WESTERN COMMERCIAL COMPANY of British Columbia built the first Skeena River salmon cannery in 1876. Located on the north end of the Inverness Slough, next to a mining camp called Woodcock's Landing, North Western produced its first pack (3,000 tall cans of red spring) the following summer. Over the next hundred years, no fewer than thirty companies operated salmon canneries near or around the mouth of the Skeena River, processing millions of fish and employing thousands of workers. All of this came to an end, however, in the summer of 1983, when the last active Skeena River cannery fell into receivership and subsequently folded. *Company Town* is the story of one such cannery.

The Raskell Packing Company (Raspaco) was, in many ways, a typical Skeena River cannery. Although no systematic survey has ever been done on what constitutes a 'typical' Skeena River cannery, there are a number of recurring patterns extant in most of the Skeena River cannery towns during the peak years of fish production. By looking at a few key variables—capital investment, ethnic division of labour, technological innovation, social organization—one can gain a better understanding of how these patterns affected the lives of workers living in these towns.

Although it has been said that the Skeena River canning industry developed independently, it was the growth of foreign capital that shaped and ultimately destroyed cannery life on the Skeena. This is a bold proposition to be sure, but it does hold true when one considers the forces at work. For example, while local commission merchants financed the first fish production facilities, after successfully utilizing their trade connections to sell the fish in England, it was not long before British companies, sensing a good opportunity, invested in these facilities to the point where they, too, were building their own salmon canneries. In concert with investment by Canadian-based Fraser River canners, the acceleration of British investment (around 1900) not only pushed out minority American interests but also resulted in numerous company consolidations and many cannery shutdowns. Naturally, these shutdowns did not occur overnight; if one considers that, during the 1920s, there were as many as eighteen canneries operating on the Skeena, and that twenty-five years later there were only four, one can understand how fleeting employment was in these fly-by-night cannery towns.

During Raspaco's final year there were just over a hundred cannery workers employed on the Skeena—about one person for every year of canning in the region. Interesting, too, was that the division of labour at Raspaco had changed little over the last century—eighty percent was Native Indian, eleven percent Chinese, five percent Japanese, and about two percent white. Over half the labour force was made up of women. Ironically, none of the labour employed at Raspaco or any of the other Skeena River canneries was from the immediate area. The entire labour force, which often comprised up to three generations of families, migrated to the canneries every summer.

The advent of technology led to a decline in labour-intensive activity. One of the main innovations—and perhaps the most despicable—was the 'Iron Chink.' Developed by E.A. Smith in 1903, it was advertised as a device that would eliminate the work of Chinese butchers, although butchering was done equally by Chinese and Native workers. While the 'Iron Chink' did eliminate butchering labour, because of its fequent breakdowns and shoddy output it is debatable whether or not it was an asset to production. The bulk of jobs lost during this time was due to the changeover to gas and diesel boats, automated canning machines, pressure cooking retort ovens, and shrink-wrapping can palletizers.

Perhaps the most intriguing aspect of Skeena River cannery life was its social structure. Cannery towns resembled feudal manors, with commission merchants such as Robert Cunningham, the man who literally created the town of Port Essington, acting as paternalistic overseers. Fishermen rented company boats and purchased company gear, while their families, who worked in the canneries, obtained credit at the company stores. All expenditures were deducted from the paycheque.

Once again Raspaco provides the model—a dynastic family overseeing an indentured population of workers. New employees would immediately be struck by the manor-like monolith of the company town. Huge wooden and corrugated metal structures towered over the river. A massive dock, supported by gigantic fir pilings, jutted from the mud flat. A road leading off the dock onto shore divided the well-kept cottages of the white managers from the ramshackle housing built for the Native and Asian workers. Over this the urbane Raskell family presided, spreading goodwill in the form of conciliatory small talk and five-dollar loans.

Raspaco differed from other cannery towns in its longevity, particularly in light of its unwillingness to operate as a modern cannery. Foreign interest, which contributed to the development of Raspaco, was quickly bought out by the independent-minded Raskells, only to be courted again in the early 1970s. (Japanese investors, who controlled 49% of the company, contributed to Raspaco's downfall by refusing to cover expenditures during British Columbia's restraint period.) Although resistant to modern technology, when the plant eventually did update its equipment, it maintained most of its labour and did not see any significant increase in production. With respect to labour relations, it was likely Raspaco's paternalistic attitude that allowed it to ignore the poor living conditions and other legitimate grievances of their non-white workers. And, despite the efforts of the United Fishermen and Allied Workers Union, and the Native Brotherhood, the unions to which the workers belonged, the labour force remained ambiguous at best.

A good part of my adolescence was spent living in a cannery town similar to Raspaco. Every summer I travelled north to the Skeena River, lived in a company bunkhouse, ate in a company cookhouse, and worked eighteen hours a day six days a week on the company dock. At the end of the season, after the psychologically debilitating sockeye run, I would begin to dream of how I would spend my earnings. Usually the dreams would involve living a life—any life—as far removed from the cannery as possible.

Halfway through my last year of work my dreams began to change. What was once a summer of 'hell for dollars' became a significant part of my life. Although I had grown up in the fishing industry, I had never thought of making it a career until then. I thought about working year round—salmon in the summer, herring in the winter—and I thought about the friends I'd made, and about what it would be like working with them while the snow was in the trees. . . . But these dreams were never to materialize, for the recession of the 1980s dealt the industry a devastating blow, and the company I grew up with closed its doors forever.

Company Town is a fictitious record of a unique time and place in British Columbia history, and of a once-vibrant industry struggling to deal with the changes of time and tide. It is also about the workers who put their hearts and souls into jobs that yielded relatively little in the way of financial reward, and who experienced racism and abuse in the light of technological innovation. They are people I grew to respect in what was a very unique community, and it is for them that this book is written.

GETTING CALLED

Getting Called

HEY YOU!
In green.
Ever punched a clock before?
Take an apron from the hanger.
There's gloves beside the dressing table.

How To Dress A Salmon

Pre-graded, right?
No pew marks, seal bites,
net marks, back breaks?
Okay.
Now put the knife in.
Here.
Good.
Just the tip.
Take the tail.
Right.
Now push-pull it.
Stop.
Flip it.
Good.
Now pass it on.

Pulling the gill.
Now you can use more knife.
Here.
Turn the head, not the blade.
Good.
Now, where's the gill?
Comes off like a ring, right?
Good.
Now pass it on.

Reaming it.
You have to cut the membrane.
See.
Cut that.
Good.
Now you rip.
Hear that pop?

Okay.
Good.
Now leave it for the washers.

The Washers'll Wash It

There's ten of 'em.
Real young.
All from the canning lines.
They're here 'cause their work's too slow.
They drive the older women crazy.

But I get 'em working.
Out here's too close.
Ev'ryone knows so'n'so.
An' no one's slow.
Out here we go one speed.

Your Quality Grader

The guy at the end there. Billy.
Ev'ry fish in the shed Billy touches.
He's looking for things
like belly burn or loose bones.
See him counting scales?
Hey, Billy, most of this is dog shit, eh?

My Job

I'm paid to watch an' work.
I'm the charge-hand.
I'm union an' the foreman's my boss.
If you're having problems
I'll let you know.
So don't go running to the foreman.
I'm your boss and I'll do that.

Five Orientations

i.

No one's from here, ya know.
Not so deep.
People come up from Kitwanga,
Kitkatla, Kispiox, the Nass. . .
Just the tip, eh?
Ninety percent of the labour's native.
Another five are Japanese.
There's a gang of Chinamen, you,
two Slavs, then me.
Right.

ii.

The G.M. flies up on weekends.
Hold the tail.
He rents an apartment in Rupert,
talks to the foreman, looks around,
flies south for Sunday dinner.
There's a bookkeeper, a secretary,
and a Red Cross lady.
Cut yet?

iii.

Payday's Friday.
Your work today's forwarded
to the next pay period.
Keeps you from taking a walk.
Base rate's ten something.
Four hundred hours you get a raise.
Thousand hours you get thirteen.
Labour Day they lay us off.
We miss UI by a week.

iv.

Red Cross lady's a gas. Miranda.
Her daddy Magnus prospered
selling herring
to the cash boats. Assholes.
Sit around in suits all day
waiting to buy pregnant fish.
Uptightest bunch I ever met.
Crap their pants at a rip tide.

Miranda, though.
Company paid for her C ticket.
Magnus and her brothers burned up
one herring, the bonanza year.
Left her alone. Had no one.
Company tried to make up for it.
Looked bad at the inquest,
then got cleared by a doctor.
Magnus was a piss-tank.
Funny girl.

v.

Show me your left hand.
Take off your gloves
an' show me your left hand.
See that? You're cut.
Another hour an' the poison's
half-way up your arm.
When it hits your heart you die.

Go to the Detol sink,
soak it a minute,
then go see Miranda.
Oh, and a coffee on your way back.
Two creams, no sugar.

Red Cross Lady's Story

i.

He's an idiot.
Thinks 'cause he grew up here
he runs the goddamn show.
Well I grew up here too, ya know.
My daddy an' me are the last
of Claxton.
Tried our damnedest to keep it going.
No phone, no cars, no store. . .
Smoke?

We'd go to Rupert once a week.
Get supplies, have a beer, you know.
I'd leave him at the Belmont,
come back in time to see him glowing.
He'd put his big arms 'round the table
an' say, Yo, Miranda,
city hall in exile!

ii.

Yah, I don't care what he says.
He grew up in Osland, ya know.
His old man, Sam. What a joker.
Dad 'n' he were the best of chums.
You could hear their fights from the Glory Hole.

iii.

True story.
The night before I was born
dad 'n' Sam were docked in Simpson;
an' mom, back in Claxton,
had just begun labour.

Well, dad 'n' Sam bin playing
crib all day, nineteen back-up,
at a quarter a point, and,
the story goes, dad was down
two hundred dollars.
So dad says to Sam
double or nothing.
Of course dad had no money
an' Sam knew it.
Halfway through the game
Sam got cocky, ten pegs up.
He kept reminding dad
he expected cash on the spot
if he won.
But dad, so sure he'd win,
insured the deal: if he lost,
and if I was a girl,
I'd be engaged to Sam's first son.
Well, there were complications.
The Port Ed doctor
got delayed by bad weather,
and I was on my way out breech.
He only got there just in time
to freak out the mid-wives,
turn me, an' watch my mother
hemorrhage to death.

Next time you pass by
the company bunkhouse
take a look through the window.
You'll see a big photo
taken by Sam
of a boat load of roses
on their way back to Claxton.

Next time, okay?

ORIENTATION #6

The Iron Chink

No point in putting your gear on.
Break's in ten minutes.
C'mon, I wanna show you something.
I want you to see where the fish go.

We unload the boats with a dry suction pump.
The fish are then sorted, according to species.
Cohoe, steelhead, dogs, and springs
get sent through to us, for dressing an' freezing.
Sockeye and humps go right to the bins.

One single bin holds eight thousand pieces.
We alternate flow from one to the other,
depending on what we are canning.
A hydraulic door joins up to a hopper,
dumping the fish in a gated container.

The fish are hand-steadied,
indexed for beheading,
then sent down the chain
to the pullers and reamers.
What's left of the fish is fed
through the bull rings; they're spat out
for sliming, five thousand per hour.

Years ago this was labour intensive.
A line of Chinese would butcher forever,
cutting down fish with two foot machetes.
As racism grew an' the companies prospered,
machines were invented to do all the dressing.
Suppose you can guess why they're called Iron Chinks?

THE "IRON CHINK"

"The Canner's Faithful Friend"

Company Store and Storekeep

Coffee's a buck.
I know it's a lot but
to ship it's a killer,
a real bitch.

Some trucks won't even come out here.
Twice last year the road caved in.
Supplier told us insurance
won't permit loads past Port Ed.
Company has to hire its own guy.

Imagine: two trips a day
in a volkswagen bug.

Okay, so that's a coffee,
a cup, two creams, no sugar.
Grand total: one fifty.
Bring back the cup and I'll give you a quarter.

Absolutely The Worst Job In The Plant

If you follow the belts
up over your head
you'll notice the fish
end up on those tables.

And under the gears
near the clincher an' seamer
you'll notice the women
who scrape for a living.

The wives an' the daughters
of the Captain Highliners
who tidy the fish
not just to pass time,

like the G.M. says,
but to pay for the gas
to get them all back
from a summer of fun at Raspaco.

ORIENTATION #8

Where The Flesh Meets The Metal

Then again to the hopper
for a trip through the knives,
to the filling machines,
to the salter and onwards,

to the patching tables,
where the gaps in the cans
are plugged an' sent on
to the seamer, the clincher,

an' the guy with the ballcap,
the bussie, who pushes his cart
right to the door of
this thing called a retort.

An' the retort cooks the fish.
An' the cans are left to cool.
And once they are cooled
they're lifted by magnets

an' stacked on to pallets,
shrink-wrapped in lots,
bought, sent off in trucks
an' that there's the whistle

so let's go. Ten o'clock.

Coffee Break

The donuts we're dipping
were packaged by Weston's.
Weston's, of course, now own
B.C. Packers; and they, of course,
can half of the fish.

For the past seven years
no one's made money.
Companies run on the strength
of their bank loans.
An' when they expand
it's with foreign investment.

In a couple of years
it'll be all over.
The small independents
will sell out to Weston's,
who'll soak up the loss
just to eat up the rest.

Yep. Long before Weston's,
and the Nelsons before them,
you could travel the Skeena
by company boardwalk.

When Magnus was born,
way back in the twenties,
there were over a dozen
companies canning.
Places like Standard, Haysport,
Claxton, Balmoral. . . .
All of them broke now
except for Raspaco.

The Storekeep

The Raskell Packing Company was founded in 1904 by John Clark Raskell, a former sea captain in the British Navy. He came to Victoria with his Canadian wife, Cruella. Her father was a partner of one of the Fraser River Ladners, an' he lent ol' Jack ten thousand dollars to open a salmon cannery on the Skeena River. Raskell left his posting on Vancouver Island an' built a house in Port Essington. It was from there that he oversaw the construction of Raspaco.

The original cannery had an office, a boathouse, segregated housing, a small store, and a hundred workers. Ev'rything was done manually. There was no Iron Chink back then. No filling machine. All the cans were hand-soldered, packed into boxes two at a time.

When my father came to work here in the early thirties me an' Jack Jr. were roughly the same age, twelve or so. My old man used to run the gas skow, an' I used to help him. Jackie used to hang around down there, as did most of the other wharf rats. We used to take turns pumping gas. Made a genuine game out of it, ya know. Dad used to drink pretty heavy back then.

A lot of changes were made once Jackie took over. The war had just ended an' Jackie was all excited about the new machines. A 9A filling machine 'came available, so Jackie 'n' me drove down to Portland an' picked one up. Same with the clinchers an' seamers, which is what we use to close the cans. Soon we added a reform line. 'Course you can't actually buy these machines; they're all leased out by the American Can monopoly. But the Iron Chink, the Iron Chinks can be bought. An' we did eventually buy one. We also bought a quonset hut off an American base in Port Ed, an' had it floated down to serve as a new tool shop. Then we built a new boat house, the old one getting converted into a new store. Jackie asked me to manage the new store, an' I've bin there ever since. Thirty years this September.

Silas Reardon From Aiyansh

The Raskell Packing Company started up in the summer of 1900, an' my father was one of the first the old man hired on. My father used to pew fish off the packers for two dollars a day. No pumps or brailers back then, eh? My mother used to wash fish. So did my sisters, Violet and Dorinda. My brother Miles an' me, we worked in the net loft, patching nets. Miles died a few years back; but I stayed on an' prob'ly will 'til I die, too.

Most of the fishermen come out from the Nass, Skeena Crossing, Hazelton, Kitkatla. Some people live in Port Ed. No one comes from Rupert, eh? Kitkatla fishermen tie up on the south floats; Nass and Japanese on the north floats. White men all over. Bin that way since day one at Raspaco.

Same with the housing. Natives and Orientals in the village, on the north side; Whites on the south side. Used to be that the village was just a bunch of tents. Then the company built a few houses ev'ry few years. White side housing got looked after. Native and Oriental side didn't. I don't know where this company'd be without us, not the other way around. Prob'ly nowhere.

Before Raspaco ev'rything was up river, eh? That was well before Rupert an' the railroad—yah, ev'rything was up river like Port Essington back then. A cumshewa named Cunningham came out an' tricked the steamship company into believing that they could sell stuff where Port Essington was even though nobody lived there yet. That was how Port Essington started an' got to be real big before the railway came along an' moved ev'rything into Prince Rupert.

The Red Cross Lady

The Raskell Packing Company began operating in 1894 or 5. John Raskell used to be a big-wig in the British Army, then got thrown out for some scandal or the other. Anyway, the government paid him off an' he came to the Skeena, where he worked as an agent for the HBC.

After a couple of years he met a rich gal from Vancouver an' built Raspaco. Their only child, Jackie, was real smart—real handsome, too. There's a big picture of him up in the office. 'Parently Jackie had quite a reputation 'round these parts. My aunt Patty used to call him the Cock of the Walk. Ha! Ha! Yah, ol' Jackie settled down eventually an' married Muriel Preston, the prettiest girl in Claxton. Dad 'n' Sam used to fight over her as kids; but deep down they and ev'ryone else knew she 'n' Jackie'd get hitched, which was prob'ly the best thing anyway. Dad 'n' Sam didn't really care too much for Jackie, though. He was a nice guy, but he didn't care too much for unions. I can see how that would piss 'em off.

When Jackie eventually took over, he decided to go out an' modernize. Trouble was he didn't know where to start. He knew nothing about machinery. Nothing about the markets. One thing he did know, though, was how to relate to the natives. And he knew his fish. You might say he had fish savvy.

Larry Woodcock had fish savvy, too. But he also knew how to operate a fish cannery. Jackie, Art Sakic, an' Larry pretty much ran things here 'til the late 1960's. Then it got too much for them. They hired a bunch of whiz kids from Vancouver, then formed Raspaco Management. A couple of months later, after Larry died, Raspaco Management sold 49% of the company to a Japanese firm. The Japanese must've paid millions and all they wanted was the rights to buy the fish eggs. Can you imagine? It seems like only yesterday we were usin' those eggs for trout bait.

The Charge-Hand

The Raskell Packing Company came about in 1901, the year
of the Fraser River fishermen's strike. John Raskell's father-in-
law made a killing screwing fishermen out of thousands of
dollars. Most of those profits were used to pay local natives
crap wages to build this cannery.

When my dad came to work here in the 1930's there was no
UFAWU. What there was, though, was a bunch of little unions
like the SPSU and the PCFU. Almost none of the shoreworkers
were organized. A lot of the native workers belonged to the
Native Brotherhood, which has always stayed separate; while
the Japanese belonged to the AFA. Magnus 'n' dad spent a
good part of their lives working toward a united union.
Miranda's granny, too. When she was a floor lady down south
she got fired for joining the FCRPWU. Spent the rest of her life
organizing for the UFAWU. And when the UFAWU did come
about, right at the end of World War II, there was a bigger
party for the union than there was for the armistice.

The union presence never got strong here, though. There's a
lot of instances where workers with legitimate grievances
didn't do anything about it. That's where Jackie was so clever.
He'd get wind of a problem, then cosy up to whoever was
pissed off. The matter would usually come down to
somebody's loss of hours when they could least afford it. A
common sight would be Jackie and the griever standing on the
office steps. The griever would be smiling and Jackie'd be dip-
ping into his wallet to lend out a twenty.

Yah, the way this place grew up has bin pretty backwards.
Fishermen and their fam'lies, as usual, end up paying for
ev'rything—housing, boats, gear, ev'rything. They also get
gouged at the company store. The whole village economy is a

reaction to that. A mixture of old ways and the ways of the white world. No potlatch—just black markets bartering on credit.

FRESH FISH

Fresh Fish

i.

In case you're wonderin',
in case you're asked,
you work in fresh fish.
You're a butcher;
but I expect you
to grade, weigh fish,
an' drive the fork-lift.
Once you've learned all that
you're laughin'.

Fresh fish is a privilege
—and a punishment.
Senior ladies like it
'cause it's quiet
an' they get more work
when they need it.
New girls hate it
'cause of the pace;
but mainly 'cause it's one
step closer to the road.

I like to keep it small.
Always more women than men.
Women work better together;
they laugh an' joke,
but it doesn't affect their hands.
You can take the same joke,
give it to the men,
and instead of laughter
you get a fist fight.

ii.

I've bin here from the start.
That was six years ago.
The company used to can ev'rything,
then opened a fresh fish shed
when the markets changed.
We started with dogs,
springs, an' cohoe;
then moved on to sockeye.
I used to work the tally-shack.
Miranda was the slitter.
Her brothers Stew 'n' Roddy
used to gill an' ream.
We had two washers.
Billy was the grader.

Before fresh fish
I fished with Magnus.
When my father died
he left me 'n' mom
a dock and half a seiner.
I sold a quarter
back to Magnus
an' moved my mom
to Hazelton.
It was all so bloody complicated.
A condition of the deal
had me crew as mate
the following five herrings.
I refused to go four years ago
an' sure enough the boat blew up.
Miranda still won't talk to me.

Waiting For Fresh Fish

They're unloading a boat from 2 West.
No sockeye. Just cannery pinks.
It'll be an hour before we see anything.
Lucky to get a few dogs.

There's one more boat after that,
but it's not in 'til three.
That'll be the CR II.
Dad 'n' Magnus had the Cathy R,
the one that went down.

Miranda has a share in CR II.
So do I. It's a three-way split.
The other partner is Art Sakic,
the guy who runs the company store.

CR II

CR II is a fifty foot
D license wood packer.
She's got a 70,000 pound
hold capability,
a General Motors
453 diesel engine,
and a re-built
Isuzu auxiliary.
It's outfitted with
four hydraulic winches,
Wagner auto, SSB,
VHF, two Lorans,
Mark II radar,
computer plotting,
and a Black Box.

The boat was bought
with a combination
of monies from
insurance, lawsuits,
and inheritances.
Miranda inherited
the money from Magnus.
Art sued the plant
'cause his son died aboard.
And I was insured
for the loss of my shares.
Nobody actually worked
to buy it. That's why
nobody wants to work her.

We hired a crew
from South Vancouver,
a bunch of kids
off the Fraser River.
They work too hard,
they never screw up,
an' they save their pay
for their educations.
The money we make
goes right to the bank,
to pay off the debt
that keeps the thing floating.

ORIENTATION #9

Still Waiting

Of the totes you'll be scrubbing
half of 'em were made
by me and Allan Sakic.
We had two weeks one year
to make fifty white totes.
As a carpenter I suck,
but Allan was no better.
He'd get the scariest slivers ever.
Packed it in at thirty
to go fishing with ol' Magnus.

ORIENTATION #10

. . . and waiting. . .

Art Sakic.
Ev'rybody loves Art Sakic.
JCR Sr. loved Art Sakic so much
he sent him down south
for his schooling.
I don't know if Art is as smart
as he's loyal
or as loyal as he's smart.
Does a good job bull-shitting
'bout how cool
the Raskell's were, though.
Tell me something.
If he's so bloody smart,
what's he doing in the company store?
Or get this: if he's as loyal
as he thinks he is,
why then did he sue the company?

ORIENTATION #11
. . . and waiting

Allan Sakic was my best friend
an' now he's fuckin' dead.

Keep scrubbin'.

A Change of Bandages

He's had a bad life.
Sam was an asshole.
Dad had a better idea
of how to treat him, though,
so you can see why
he got all bitter when dad died.
Still won't talk to me.

He tends to flip out on down time,
waiting for a fish boat.
He'll prob'ly knock off an hour—
take a walk, maybe a nap.
If you need any help,
if you're wanting for something,
go see a guy by the name of
Dean Reardon.

Dean Reardon

The Raskell Packing company hired me in the summer of 1967. I was fixing cars at the time, over in the village, for a couple of bucks an hour. My cousin's brother-in-law, Abel Drew, was plant foreman, and he needed an assistant lineman for the quarter-pound line.

I'd never worked so hard in my life. The linemen were all qualified millwrights and I was this hack mechanic. I learned enough in three months to get hired back as filling machine man.

Five years ago they asked me if I wanted to be foreman. I had to think about it—thought about it a whole week. Thought it might be too tough, considering the fact I'd be bossing my own people around. But, hey, I figured since I was only part white it wouldn't be much of a problem.

Doing What Dean Says

After you finish with the totes
I want you to help Joe
in the ice house.
Here, I'll show ya.

Water is frozen up top, eh,
like rain is to snow,
except the water
comes out in chips.
A mechanical rake
plows the ice
to an augur,
which carries it up
through a shaft to a chute.
The black button
is for loading boats.
The yellow button
is for loading totes.
The green button
starts the rake.
If something screws up
push the red one.

The problem is the rake.
It's broken.
I want you 'n' Joe
to pile ice in the augur.
Under no circumstances
do you stay inside
while the augur's on.
Just load 'er up.
Get out.
Clear it.

Then get back in
an' do it again.
I've got two boats
in at three,
and I want them out
by four.

What Joe Says

I love it here.
I've bin here ev'ry summer
for the past six years.
Look forward to coming back
each spring.
I've worked at other canneries,
but this one's easily the best.
Ya know why?
'Cause nobody gives a shit.
I mean the work gets done, right?
The union's always there for us,
an' management's real passive.
Ev'ryone knows their job,
so what's the problem?

I'll tell you what's the problem.
Take the guy in fresh fish,
the charge-hand.
He gets paid to fuck the dog.
But what does he do?
The complete opposite!
He worries.
Worries like a bookkeeper.
Spends way too much time
actually working.
Working for what? The company?
He hates the company!
You should see him
at study session.
It's like he's plotting
an expropriation.
A burn-out if I've ever seen one.

Most people are like me.
They punch in, do their job,
then punch out again.
The trick is how you pass the time.
Like right now.
You don't think about the boats
needing ice for their fish.
You think about the ice,
what it was before.
You think about the water.
Where does it come from?
It comes from the dam,
up in the mountains.
Ever bin up there?
It's beautiful.
Big trees, wild flowers.
But even before that,
up in the sky.
Think about the water.
See it floating, a mist,
forming into droplets.
See all this happen, the cycle.
Water, ice, water, ice.
Hey. Do you believe in god?

Lunch On The Charge-Hand

Ev'rything is overpriced.
Whatta scam they've got themselves.
Ingrid drives the hotdog truck;
her sister Mary runs it.
They get their food
from the company store
an' cook it in the parking lot.
Bin doin' that for thirty years,
since Mary married Arthur Sakic.

Art Sakic on Dean

Silas Reardon's his grandfather.
He's a big man back home,
but out here he fixes nets.
His father's Maurice.
Maurice is a highliner,
but back home he's an infidel.
Dean's the plant foreman.
Anywhere else he's Silas' grandson.

Red Cross Lady On Art Sakic

Art Sakic is Raspaco.
Lives here all year 'round, ya know.
Absolutely no question you'll ever
meet a man who knows more
'bout this river
or is more loyal to this plant
than Art Sakic.
Never have I heard him say
one bad word about this place
or anyone around it.
No, sir.
But hey. You'd better be careful.
Art Sakic is one man
who's very tough to trust.

Dean On The Red Cross Lady

Oh, she's had a bad life.
Lost her mom at birth,
dad 'n' two brothers in a boat fire.
You'd never know it, though.
No one loves life like Miranda.

Art On The Charge-Hand

Strange bird, that one.
I've watched him grow up,
and he grew up funny.
Moody, moody, moody.
An' totally unpredictable.
You'll never figure him out.
And I'm a good judge of people.
Trust me on that one.

CANNERY CUT

Four Totes Of Chum

You know the season's gettin' on
when you get fish like this up.
Hudson Bay blankets we call 'em.
Ever seen a Hudson Bay blanket?
Chock full of colour just like these here dogs.
They're okay to smoke, but that's about it.
We'll dress these for canning.
Too big for the bull rings.

Cannery Cut

Rather than take the gill out
we'll just cut the head off.
You put the knife under these fins, see,
an' saw on an angle
a couple of inches.
Now flip it on over.
The same thing but this way.
Right.
Off comes the head.

Take the tail an' slit from the hole.
Right through to the end.
Now ream it like sockeye.
Good.
Take off the fins.
Good.
Okay.
Still too big.
Now comes the tough part.

There's a number of ways
to fillet a fish.
You can start at both ends.
I start at the tail.
Now press the knife flat
'til you feel out the backbone.
Gently saw in
where the skin bulges over.
Follow the bone right up to the neck.
Good.
Good.
STOP.
You're losing the meat.

Here.
There.
Flip it again.
Now do it all over.
Okay.
Three pieces.
Two of meat,
one of bone.

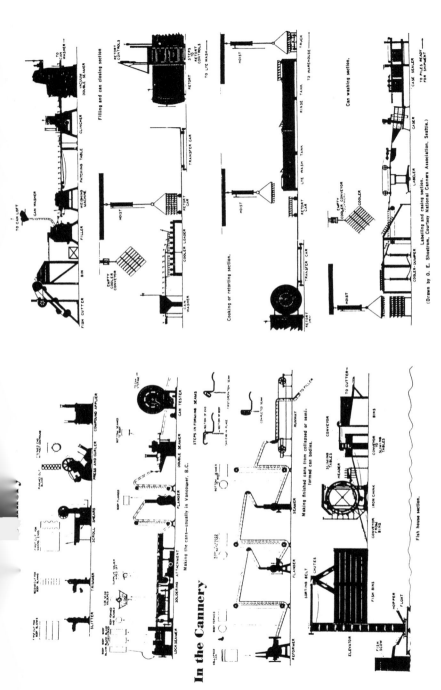

In the Cannery

Making the cans—usually in Vancouver, B.C.

Making finished cans from collapsed or semi-formed can bodies.

Fish house section.

Filling and can closing section.

Cooking or retorting section.

Can washing section.

Labelling and closing section.
(Drawn by O. E. Shostrom. Courtesy National Canners Association, Seattle.)

A Fish By Any Other Name

The Feds call them chum.
Americans, king salmon.
We know them as dogs
or Hudson Bay blankets.
There wasn't much call
for these fish in the old days.
Threw them all back
whenever they caught one.
Not red enough
for the picky consumer.

Same for the white spring.
Threw them back, too,
'til someone came up
with a marketing scheme:

WHITE SPRING SALMON
GUARANTEED NOT TO TURN RED IN THE CAN

Pretty stupid, eh?

ORIENTATION #13
Way Back They'd Limit Humps

Way back they'd limit humps.
Said they couldn't can that fast.
Bullshit.
Companies feared a market glut,
so they conspired on a price fix.
Man, there was so much waste
in those days.
People starving an' good food
floating dead in the rivers.

A Fish By Any Other Name Again

A couple more things.
Humps are pinks.
They're called humps 'cause
their backs arch up
when they get near spawning.
Small springs are jacks.
Big springs tyee.
Big tyee are what anglers want;
but if you ask me
the best fish for flavour are cohoe.
Americans don't know that, though.
They come up with their rods
an' their bottles of beer,
looking for the big score.
Never known one sportsman
to actually eat his catch.
They'd either chuck 'em or mount 'em.

Steelhead, Too

There's another fish we dress out here.
The steelhead.
They're classed as a trout,
but they look more like salmon.
Any steelhead we can't freeze
get sent off for cannin',
where they pack them as red spring.
By the year 2000 there might be none left.
Can't throw them back
once they're dead in the net.
Sportsmen won't part with them
if they're too big.
The only thing left
is the hatchery.

I knew of these guys,
a couple of Feds,
who worked on the test boat
down by Tyee.
Scientist types
who walked an' talked steelhead.
Used to tie flies
an' make their own liquor.
Late in the sixties
they caught wind of Harry,
an ass of a man
who fished out of season.
According to the story
this guy was out seining
an' lost half his net
'cause the herring were diving.
Got all pissed off
an' jumped in his dinghy,

rowed up a creek
with a box full of seal bombs.
Blew out two hundred
immature steelhead,
then sold them for gear
to a Port Edward smoker.
Word soon got 'round
an' these two Federalies
tracked Harry down
to a pub in Prince Rupert.
They got him pissed drunk
on government money,
then took him out back
for a serious beating.
Left him in traction
with a plate for a forehead.

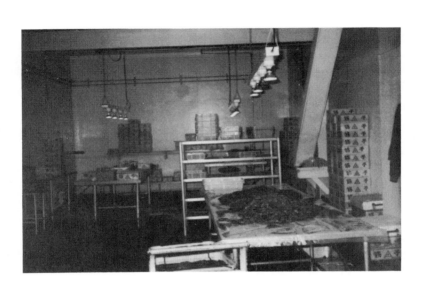

Where The Eggs Go

Sockeye, pink,
spring, an' chum
all yield good eggs.
Steelhead eggs are useless, though.
Too small and unattractive.

We weigh the eggs,
then send them off
to a room for agitation.
Each roe is graded,
one by one, then packed
in little boxes.

The company that does all this
is run by Japanese.
They bought up half
Raspaco's shares
for first rights on the product.

All the eggs
are shipped on out
to brokers in Japan.
They're auctioned off
to restaurants
who use them to make sushi.

Company Bunkhouse

I remember once
I got some eggs
an' took them
to the bunkhouse.
All the guys
were partied up
an' getting pretty hungry.
We ended up
in Bobby's room
with a box of
wheat thin crackers.
Ev'ryone threw up
that night,
except for Joe Tanaka.

Billy Dayton In Fresh Fish

The Raskell Packing Company employed my family for years.
I started at fifteen on the back of the gut skow. Company used
to dump all the fish guts. Then the Feds came 'round—said it
broke down the food chain.

At the end of the day we'd get towed down the river, to a
reduction plant at North Pacific. They used all the fish guts to
make dog food an' vitamins. Now all the waste is sent out in
trucks.

When they sold off the gut skow they asked me to work on
The Chink. Bobby Geary used to feed it, an' he used to let me
do it a couple of times. When Bobby left for the Co-op, I
became the feeder. Used to feed it at a hundred and twenty
fish per minute. One of the linemen timed me.

I moved over to grader a few years ago 'cause the noise was
too much for me. It's real quiet over here. Besides, I like
touching fish that aren't torn to hell.

Export

Write up a tag.
Write:

Put it on that buggy there,
and wheel it to the freezer.
You'll work for Eddie 'til coffee.

Eddie's Freezer And Cold Storage

A pan has two pieces.
Four sides as one
and a bottom.
Easier to clean that way.
These fish are big, +9s,
so we'll use up the large pans.
Two to a pan, eh.
This way, like ying-yang.
Now use the stool
an' shelf it up top.
Work down from there.

Done already?
Okay, now place a tag
on the last row you did
an' follow me back
to the cold room.
We've got sockeye to glaze.

When we strip the freezers
we take fish from the pans
an' put them in totes.
The fish are then moved
to the back with a hand-jack,
where we prepare them
for glazing, strapping, an' boxing.
We then dip the fish
in a sugar solution,
an' bag them in plastic
three at a time.
They're stuffed into boxes
an' sent down the roller,
where Jonesy is waiting

with his strapping machine.
Each box of three,
at +6 per fish,
should weigh no more
than twenty-two pounds.
That's eighteen for fish,
two for the box,
an' one for the glaze
that keeps us in profit.

Freezer Labour

The kids working here.
All of 'em drifters.
Quebecois, Albertans,
one guy from Cleveland.
Most of the labourers
come from the area.
Children of children
way back to day one.
Not these guys, though.
The senior-most worker
has bin here one paycheque.

Eddie Singletary

The Raskell Packing Company hired me out of retirement two years back. I knew the old man when I had MacEwan's. We were in competition back then. Anyway, Jackie wanted to put in a fresh fish shed. Eventually he realized that with a fresh fish you need a freezer.

In the beginning they used to salt the fish. Used to salt 'em in great big barrels. 'Course the natives had bin salting, drying, an' smoking fish for years. No money in salt fish now.

Makes a lot of sense having a frozen product. Problem is ev'ryone's so particular about what makes a good fish. Can't have no pew holes, belly burn, net marks, all that crap. Read somewhere where the Feds don't want too much fresh fish on the market 'cause it causes lay-offs in canning. Bullshit. It's the buyers from Japan—they want a fish like it fell from the sky.

Yah, so I'll give it a while longer. What the hell, eh? I'm seventy years old an' bored shitless.

Plant __Raspaco Skeena__   Date __Aug. 30, '83__

Species __Cohoe__   Tally # __1/3__

+ 9 EX.	6 - 9 EX.	- 6 EX.
3 x +9	3 x 6-9	4 x -6
3 x +9	3 x 6-9	4 x -6
3 x +9	3 x 6-9	4 x -6
3 x + 9	3 x 6-9	4 x -6
3 x +9	3 x 6-9	4 x -6
3 x +9	3 x 6-9	
3 x +9	3 x 6-9	
3 x + 9	3 x 6-9	
3 x + 9	3 x 6-9	
3 x + 9	3 x 6-9	
5 x + 9	3 x 6-9	
3 x + 9	5 x 6-9	
3 x + 9	3 x 6-9	
3 x + 9	3 x 6-9	
5 x + 9	3 x 6-9	
3 x + 9	3 x 6-9	
3 x + 9	3 x 6-9	

E Singletary

Tallyman's signature

3pm Tally Sheets

Not a bad day today.
Two thousand pieces of #1 export.
Take the tallies to Mary,
then go for coffee.
We'll see you back here
for a couple more hours.

Secretary Mary

The Raskell Packing Company has taken care of my family for
years. My grandfather used to fish for Raspaco back in the
days when the fish boats had sails. An' my grandmother, she
used to stack cans in steam boxes long before seamers an'
clinchers. My father fished the Raspaco 6 for thirty years, with
me an' my sisters dressing fish on the bow. When I graduated
from high school Jackie offered me the secretary job. That
was. . . well. . . a few years ago anyway.

Two Pieces Of Paper To Pass On To Peter

Here is your tax form
and a union thing.
Under ESTIMATED EARNINGS
add what monies
you've made since April
plus enough to keep you
under exemption.
For the union thing
just sign your name.

Peter Rhodes From West Vancouver

The Raskell Packing Company had a job description at UBC manpower a few years back. I was just finishing a B.A., in philosophy, wondering what the hell I was gonna do next, when I phoned. The company wanted a commerce grad, so I lied at the interview. When they showed me the job I almost blew it. I mean, I almost broke out laughing. Any six-year-old could have done the kind of books they wanted done. Yah, an' they were looking for a B.Comm.

A Look In The Books

Check this out.
Last year's highliner,
landing 5,000 sockeye,
finished the season
two grand in debt.

An' last years low man,
who caught one hundred sockeye,
came away from this place
with nine hundred dollars.

The End Of The Road

I grew up in West Van, ya know.
Prob'ly wonderin' what the hell
I'm doing out here, on the Skeena.
Well. This is the end of the road, right?
Look at Mary.
Couldn't get a job in Prince Rupert.
Ev'ryone knows she spent time
in Essondale.
Tried to do a hatchet job
on her husband,
a man they called The Mink.

I'm from one of those dynasties.
Ya know what I mean?
Beautiful people, lots of money.
Come from a long line of realtors.
Supposed to be a lawyer or a doctor,
not some ticket punch on the Skeena River.
Yep. This is it.
End of the fuckin' road.
I love it.

3pm Coffee: Silas Reardon

Look at them dogs.
You'll never see dogs
like that in town, eh.
Any dog that gets that ugly
gets caught by the pound
an' put down to sleep.
Yah, 'round July
when ev'ryone's rich
they go buy a car
an' some fancy mutt.
Then when they split
an' go back home
they forget all about
the dogs that they bought.
The dogs end up
up by the dam,
living off rats
an' birds that they catch.
They run in big packs
an' start interbreeding.
An' the pups that aren't eaten
grow up just as ugly.
One time while driving
I saw a real monster:
head like Chihuahua,
body like a collie,
legs super fat
like one of them pit bulls.
Pulled the truck over
and pulled out my Nikon,
a couple of miles
past Sunnyside.

3pm Coffee: Dean Reardon

See those three guys.
They're the linemen.
Most important cog
in the wheel 'round here.
When the lines are up
they go unnoticed.
But when things break down
they're all you see.

Take the half-pound line.
Thousands of parts
in the AmCan catalogue,
knocking together
to kick out a can.
And of all the parts
that make up the lines,
well over half
aren't even in stock.

When the lines go down
it gets acrobatic.
Linemen with wrenches
an' big rubber hammers
flat on their backs
an' jumping off ladders;
or bent over benches
with tiny screwdrivers,
then bolting for the clincher
with some home-made contraption.

I remember one week
the lines were just perfect.
An' Bud, the G.M.,

was up with his wife.
As pay day came 'round
he was signing the cheques
when the linemen came in
to pick up their pay.

Ol' Bud blew up
when he added their totals.
He said, Thirty grand
just to sit an' watch cans!
And young Bobby Dollas,
great big Bobby Dollas,
threw down his keys to say,
You start the lines.

Well, Bud took the bait.
And the very next day
he told us his wife
would turn on the lines.
He turned to walk out
then a cough and a sputter
and all of us standing there
watching our boots.

3pm Coffee: Art Sakic

Half an' quarters
of sockeye an' pink
go mostly to Britain.
Cans of cohoe
go to France.
Chum an' spring,
here 'n' there.
Frozen steelhead
go to Brooklyn.
Frozen sockeye
to Japan.
Tips 'n' tails
an' salmon mince
get canned in talls
for B.C. Ferries.
That is our last
domestic market.

3pm Coffee: The Charge-Hand

Reggie drives the reform line,
a '69 Camaro,
an' the bum leg he was born with.
He works long hours trying to
make his job easier.
When the plant shuts down
he drives to the desert,
to a cheap hotel off the Vegas strip.
I get a letter in December.
It's the same as all his other letters.
He tells me how he's up all night
counselling some old pro off booze or dope,
foretelling the day he'll be back again,
to fix those dented cans again,
so he'll never have to come back
again an' again an' again, again.

3pm Coffee: The Red Cross Lady

I just sent Todd Hooper
to the hospital.
Ripped open his hand
in the hold of a boat.
Dean asked me to tell you
to go take his place.
How 'bout that.
You're now an unloader.

WHERE THE FISH
ARE NEAR FRESHEST

Where The Fish Are Near Freshest

So, Dean tells me
you're down in the hold.
Hand-bombing fish no less.
Well, put on Todd's gear
an' we'll see you 'round supper.
Five hundred pieces of +10 dog salmon.

In The Hold With Todd's Brother, Ron

Kinda spooky, ain't it?
The cold, the dark, the slime.

ORIENTATION #16
Hand-Bombing

To pick up a fish
you pinch its neck.
None of this under
the gill stuff, okay?
If it's too heavy to lift,
then use both your hands.
One on the neck, yah,
and one on the tail.
Push from the tail,
but don't break its back.
Into the brailer they go.

ORIENTATION #17

In Between Brailers

Bin 'round this place
most of my life.
Lived in Van
for a couple of months,
with Miranda.
Had a shit hole shack,
on Dundas Street,
near the P.N.E.
Both worked a while
for Canfisco.
It was okay I guess.

I came back
an' she moved in
with this Ted guy,
a dude she met
in Prince Rupert.
He was an artsy type
who worked for the Fed,
lived down south
in the winters.

It was true love.
They were gonna get married.
Made all these plans
for the next fifty years.
Miranda got hours
working roe-herring,
Ted went fishing
with Magnus.

Ron Hooper

The Raskell Packing Company is the last operating cannery on the Skeena River. This'll prob'ly be the last year, though. Company seems to be in trouble. But whatta ya do, eh? If that free trade deal with the States goes through, Canadian fish'll be processed in Washington or Alaska anyway; so it doesn't matter whether the company folds or not. We'll all be outta work one way or the other.

My great-grandfather was one of the first employees. He was the tallyman. Made enough in his first years to build a house in Port Ed. 'Course those were the days when the road wasn't laid yet. Used to row to work an' back ev'ryday after.

My grandfather eventually tore that house down to build a bigger one. My old man put two additions on. When he goes, I dunno. I'll prob'ly stay in Rupert.

This Was A Great Place

This was a great place.
Me, Miranda and her brothers,
Stew 'n' Roddy, and Al Sakic,
the Geary sisters, Dolly 'n' Crystal,
even your boss in fresh fish,
we all ran together.

We had our own boats
like city kids had cars.
Used to all take off
for Porcher, DeHorsey,
or the Kennedy Islands,
getting loaded on beers
or mushrooms from Masset.

Good times, those were.
Then people started dying a lot.
Nobody has much to say
these days.

Finishing Early For Overtime

That's the last of it.
Got an hour or so
before supper.
There's one more boat
with a few thousand pounds,
but it won't be in
for awhile yet.
You might as well
get that hand looked at.
Seems like it's causing you grief.

Waiting For The Whistle

Not much I can do here.
You've torn it just a little deeper,
but it's still not deep enough to stitch.
All's I can do is wash it again.
Maybe try an extra butterfly.

I'm taking off a little early.
If you want somewhere
to hide from Dean
just hang out here 'til five o'clock.
Sorry I don't have any magazines.
Here, you might be int'rested in this.

Dean At The Whistle

Looks like that boat's
goin' down south.
Not much on it anyway.
Mary'll have a cheque ready.
That's it for this week.

Farewell From Art Sakic

Talked to Mary.
She'll get you petty cash.
Not much left in the way of work, eh?
They'll prob'ly close the river Tuesday.
You might try McMillan's in town.

A Lift Out From The Charge-Hand

Art tells me you're goin' to McMillan's.
Not a bad operation.
They do ev'rything by hand still.
Nothing there but quality.
Look, if you need a ride
I'm goin' to town.
Miranda's asked me in for dinner.

POEMS FOUND AT SEA

Hurricane Verseperson

Kneeling on
creased and creamy
knuckles in
the middle of a shell
midden I crushed

clam huts
abandoned crab castles
abalone palaces
all on vacation
with my breath

Hitch-Hiked

Twenty feet
in the air.

White knuckling
on a chorus of
jack hammers.

My spine:
a vertebral
pogostick

trying to escape.

The turns twist me,
contorting
the inner ivory

'til it screams.

Work Shirt

I've got a shirt
I wash at night
that never dries.

It lies half on
the window sill
and hangs half off
the heat box.

Some time at night
the wind picks up
and blows it
through the building.

I'll find it
on my way to work,
a grease rag
on some gas pump.

Sure Sign Of Fish

If a raven sets down
on the roof of a gut truck
without even picking for milts
then it's a sure sign of fish

It's a sure sign of fish
if the raven stops squawking
to pick for a milt
or a head with its eyes still in

For sure
if the raven flies off
with four eyes facing westward
then the fish will be caught
in the Inverness Slough

But if the raven is seen tonight
dressed in whale skin
we can set down our nets
for the next hundred years

7:59 A.M.

Company man stands on a tote
and thinks he's ten feet tall.
His watch extends long past the dock,
the parking lot, the hotels and motels
we wake up from.

He sees our kitchen tables.
And from our kitchen tables he sees us
flickering, grabbing for underwear,
wincing into clothes all wet with overtime.

As he drinks the coffee we don't have time for
he thinks a lot about our sleep, how we dream
of milts and roe, loose bones,
belly burn, pew holes. . .

Company man, now tippy-toed, taller
as the time grows closer, plants a thought
beneath our heads:
company clock's a moment slow.

In his eyes we know we're tardy
but stop to look and light a smoke.
He opens his mouth to bring us down.
The whistle blows, we punch in late.

Dead Labour

The boots I wear are second-hand.
They belonged to a man who worked in this plant
for forty years,
though the boots are only six months old.
I was just eighteen when I learned his job
and could only keep up in runners, then.

He had me work the tally-shack,
calling out the boats unloading, hollering
"the springs are white not red
and for godssake boy do watch your toes
'cause if you don't they'll can 'em."

                              Yah.

I've seen you on the fresh fish dock,
on your survey walk, muttering for trouble,
for someone sloughing off.
You'd tip-toe 'round
the shards of ice, the pools of blood,
to tell me I've done an o.k. job,
to keep it up and we'll all get along.

But when I ask you why I don't get paid
my predecessor's rate, you say,
"oh you don't know squid about the fish"
or "you're all wrong for this industry."
And then you mumble off again
with a "blame it on your union, son."

Abandoned Cannery

Always stunned at the ebb
your crooked legs tell me
you're more barge than building still,
as if some god overruled your evolution.

You took your stand
in the river's mouth,
stretching out your tongue
in a burlesque of Tsimshian myth.

Into your lap
you herded the souls
of your labourer's kin,
informing them that their lineage
would be better served in a soldered can.

For one hundred years
you bit this river,
chewing on your silver dollars,
and spitting out
what should have been
another perfect generation.

Company Town

i.

Born in the spark light
breaking tools make, our screams
lost out to the stripping of gears
deep in the cannery format.

Our first steps were taken
not long after, on the day-shift
march to the time-clock shelter.

But when the final whistle blew
we knew our turn may never come,
that we may figure in a wasted plan.

So we jumped the last truck out.

ii.

And the road was full of holes.
And the bumps were too much for some.
And we knew that the promise
of pavement was lost, though we clung

to the words of our driver:
the the road well-travelled
was the route worth taking.

How wrong we were already.

From the smell of melting fly-wheel
we knew our ride was dying;
and our driver, though kind enough,
was never meant to join us.

iii.

Still, we reached the city limits.
And we knew that a visit
would make us the wiser
if we carried with us where we came from.

So we took apart our transportation,
taking turns on the rusty bolts.
And with these bolts we would
soon make new ones.

We would discourse on their inner workings
and we would grind them together
to start our fires, for we knew
not what we'd broken from

but how wrong we were already.

MICHAEL TURNER was born in North Vancouver, B.C. in 1962. As a teenager, he spent his summers working in a fish cannery on the Skeena River. After graduating from the University of Victoria with a degree in anthropology, he helped form Hard Rock Miners, a Vancouver-based hillbilly band who record on the Einstein Bros./Sony label. His poems have appeared in numerous periodicals, journals, and anthologies in Canada. *Company Town* is his first book.